In her compelling debut, *The Song Around Us*, Kat Hayes stitches a rich, lyric narrative from broken images, rending music from silence and stillness from the thrashing of bird wings. So as not to be undone by a crumbling landscape fighting to take her with it, Hayes' speaker doesn't learn to survive the wreckage of an unchangeable past—she weighs the danger and damage "as far down the road as [she] can" in each direction and teaches herself to "turn everything to sound" in its absence, seeing how even rock shows the way "to be alone," which she knows is not the same as being lonely. There is grit in the machinery of this speaker's life, and through her commitment to deep looking we bear generational witness to wildness, tenderness, mourning, and hope alongside her in these lush poems.
—**LISA FAY COUTLEY,** author of *HOST* and *Small Girl*

If attention, as Paul Celan said, is the natural prayer of the soul, then Kat Hayes' *The Song Around Us* is, as she writes, "the pulse behind the chaos" of her ever-expanding past. Hayes handles the precise, untouchable details of that past as one might approach a sudden, severe wound: stunned, attentive, surprisingly steady. It's her voice—confusion coolly composed—that gives these poems their lyrical verve, heft and flight. It's not long before I realize Hayes has placed me among the particulars of her universe. I believe it all, especially when I read these poems aloud; somehow Hayes transforms my listening into a kind of singing. Hayes reminds me how there is no better news, despite it all, than this: "you should know / you can sing your way back."
—**ALEXANDER LONG**

The landscape is alluring, luminous, and terrifying in these poems. Hayes peels back objects, sounds, time, and we peep the vibrant life hiding beneath. In a visceral way she evokes the body's dance with mortality, the powerful relationship between man and animal, mother and daughter, lovers in the wild. Her gift for vivid imagery is astonishing.

Her subject matter tosses between the familiar and unfamiliar. Thoughtful, serious, and always rewarding. This book is an instant winner.
—**IHEOMA NWACHUKWU,** author of *Japa and Other Stories*

Katrina Hayes' aptly titled *The Song Around Us*, sings full-throated. Elegies, odes, narratives of coming of age in the grit-imbedded landscape of "rusted furnaces and the metal intestines of factories" are imbued with "the heart's iambic thump." Almost prayerful meditations on unspoiled nature, on the awe of a parent watching her child explore, these all hum lyrically. Some collections beg to be read in order; most are read randomly. Hayes' book rewards the reader who reads either way. Each poem is a gem to be discovered and savored, but the reader who starts with poem one and follows to the last will be rewarded by discoveries. A speaker who writes to heal her father becomes the mother who learns "from my daughter how to access the animal self." Heart-pounding rhythms follow quiet near-silences then swing back. Take the journey with Hayes, then reread favorites over and over.
—**LIZ ABRAMS-MORLEY,** author of *Beholder* and *Because Time*

The Song
Around Us

THE SONG AROUND US

Kat Hayes

SOLUM
LITERARY PRESS

Scottsdale, AZ • solumpress.com

Solum Literary Press
15850 N Thompson Peak Pkwy, 2176
Scottsdale, AZ 85260

solumpress.com

PAPERBACK ISBN 979-8-9898558-3-4
EBOOK ISBN 979-8-9898558-4-1

Cover art and design by Sarah Christolini.
Interior design by Riley Bounds and Sarah Christolini.
Author photo by Matthew Hayes.

LIBRARY OF CONGRESS CATALOGUING-IN-PUBLICATION DATA
Name: Hayes, Kat, author.
Title: The song around us / kat hayes.
Description: Scottsdale, AZ: Solum Literary Press, 2024.
Identifiers: LCCN 2024937782
ISBN: 979-8-9898558-6-5 (print)
ISBN: 979-8-9898558-7-2 (ePub)
Subjects: BISAC: POETRY / General / Subjects & Themes - Inspirational and Religious / American - General
LC record available at https://lccn.loc.gov/2024937782

For Matt, Quinn, and Isla

"During the intervening liminal period, the state of the ritual subject . . . is ambiguous; he passes through a realm that has few or none of the attributes of the past or coming state."
—Victor Turner

CONTENTS

IV. Visions

V. Miracles

Acknowledgments

Cimarron Review: "The Cyclist"; *Ecotone*: "Cabin," "How He Survived"; *Ekstasis*: "Finger Lake"; *Lake Effect*: "The Strip"; *Nimrod*: "Map Song"; *Off the Coast*: "Facing It"; *Ruminate*: "Girl Become Hawk"; *Salamander*: "The Cowshed"; *Solum Journal*: "Skunk Hollow"; *Vice-Versa, University of Hawaii*: "The Light Inside," "Split," "Two of Me."

"How He Survived" also appeared in the anthology *In The Tempered Dark* edited by Lisa Fay Coutley.

"Dear Calendula" and "The Mind is Like This" appeared in the anthology *Plant People* by *Plants & Poetry Journal*.

"County Fair" and "Midwinter Garden" appeared in the anthology *What Is All This Sweet Work?* edited by Brian Geiger.

THE SONG AROUND US

I. Rituals

The Strip

He was the boy who touched
electric fences. I split myself
apart and hardly noticed.

Nights we drove the strip
past tattoo parlors and thrift stores
with their headless manikins.

Trash was burning outside town—
lit diapers and liquor boxes
smoke-holed and fire-eaten.

We drag raced ambulances
headed to Good Samaritan.
We parked and heaved ourselves

into the Quitapahilla. I found a cow's
head cut from its body by the burn barrel
and didn't say anything.

Cliques buzzed at the Dairy Queen,
the vacancy sign's glow so ceaseless
we drove north to the station

where trains chugged coal to
Philadelphia. We flew past
 the tech school and prison,

past Fatt Boys steakhouse.
The ghosts hung over us,

blowing their steam-powered

whistles, bending their necks,
the fields churned up, the fires
glowing like sky lanterns

in the dark yards of neighbors
who had nothing except
bacon grease in coffee cans,

and wash lines hanging like
tracks over the grass,
and the preacher grandstanding.

We flung arms out windows
of Mustangs and trucks with
hunting rifles under the seats

Like my daddy done, he said.
That head had no body, I said.
Should I burn it?

We existed and did not exist.
The strip was a match
I held my hand over.

Elegy for My Hometown

Evenings I stood outside
hearing the hundreds of corn husks rustle
knowing all life was ahead of me.
Next door the cows stamped in their dark stalls,
the clouds blew past, the silo stood
like a fat minaret over the moving acres
of wheat. On Union Alley, rusted
furnaces and the metal intestines
of the factories towered above
as I drove to the high school.
The Tulpehocken Creek curved
like a scapula around the quarry
where I looked for old liquor bottles,
bodies, a lost dog leash.

Split

When we hit the dune
my liver split apart
like a fault line.
I was two,
on an ATV
with my father.
We were in Monterey,
the sand's white tracks
like thread across canvas.
After the crash,
the chopper thrashing
and thrashing the air
with its twin blades,
my cracked liver
waited in the bony hive
of my ribcage.
No one talks about this—
the night before surgery
I healed myself, the lost
mass regenerating,
the fresh cells moving
proteins, lipids,
glycogen. Without
intervention, I had
sown myself up.
I was young
when I learned to
keep myself alive.

Facing It

In the graveyard down the block
we stand beneath a massive nest.

It is impossibly heavy and fragile—
like a concave womb—stitched with twigs.

I am thinking of breakable things
high up, above the graves—
those sunken nests when life is gone.

I stand with my aunt unable to move
unable to make the stubborn tombs
any less familiar.

We know how a name
is set irrevocably in stone,
how the hyphen between two years
is a bitter pill—
a whole life reduced to

a brief, cold line
like a second epitaph.

We know the way dirt falls
slow off the shovel,
and the intolerable fact
that it is falling

Suddenly the words we say,
are like the words we engrave,
truncated, final.

And the dirt falls
with the precision
we lack for remembering.

The Everywhere

Out of the everywhere into here.
 —George MacDonald

Solar lantern glow—stored up sun
as white fluorescence,
toilet seat ring-tossed on the bonfire,
bats flapping over the dark garden
incense wedged in balsa wood,
black marshmallow, short dresses,
work boots trampling the potato bed.
The fire waned and we heaved on dead
Christmas trees—they went up like paper to ash
blown up towards the paulownia's low branches.
That day was field work, fixed gears
and fire-hot. That night was beer
and flame pulse from plastic lighters
and bullfrogs lowing and lowing in the streambed.
We shaped coals into a phoenix, and in the morning
marveled at its white body spread across the pit
where we flicked cigarettes, food scraps,
intuition, until dawn spread its wings.

No Trespassing

After that it was gun barns
and hot tractor cabs. Cutoff jeans
and suspenders. Tire swing and
crash of red-winged blackbird.
It was trucks over the mountain,
star clusters, collision of mud
and bone, skulk of foxes, disability checks.
It was bark scrape and broken porcelain,
soles skewered with fishhooks.
It was blackness of factories,
and low creeks, power out,
heron wing.

The Quarry

By the quarry I find a sweatshirt
stuffed in a trash can, its dirty hood
hung over the edge like one of Dali's
melted clocks. Two boys with their sleeves
cut off chip golf balls into water.
My stalking punctuated by plunks,
I take mind pictures, documenting
evidence for a trial not yet begun,
not even conceived of. I examine the
strangled can of Natural Ice,
the gray water at the low bank,
the cigarette packs, the abandoned
bait containers, the Big Gulp half
sunk in the shallows. Graffitied
on the rocks is the encoded
confession if I can just crack it.
A hair might be caught
on the chicory's blue petals
and the bloated truck tire
is not without message. I walk
under the flat leaves of the catalpa,
it's stringy seed pods hang down
in clusters like fingers.
The light gone slack, I head
to the pavilion. Picnic tables
chained to the concrete, wedged
candy wrappers, patch of duct tape,
yellow pollen film. On the gravel,
the double arabesque of a dead snake.

Ode to the Grappling Hook

Dragging lake bottoms, dredging up bodies,
or clawed over ledges for thieves,
leaving tine marks on sills for detectives' fingers.
Lowered from a barn beam, clutching hay.
Crow's foot flung over minefields to detect tripwires,
soldiers on their stomachs pulling back and back.
Once, I saw a man with one sunk in the black
sole of his shoe in case he had to scale
the face of a building or make a quick get-away
from a balcony. He told me how to make it:
With a Sharpie, trace the hook on the heel
of an old shoe. Dremel the pattern. Drill a hole
clear through the sole and thread the cable through.
Store the slack in your sock and wedge the hook
into the rubber trench. As necessary,
snatch back what was stolen from you.

Two of Me

Last night there were two of me—
one controlled the other.
In a train station, one lay down in a puddle
wanting an end but the other saved it
saying *sit up, sit up*. I wanted to keep
commuters from moving my body.
I wanted to board a train that never came.
For the most part I couldn't be bothered
with me. But I fumed when I lay down
in ditches every time I turned my back.
It was enough to animate one self each day—
I resented my resolute surrender,
my lack of agency, how like a drunk
I had to be cajoled and kept out of gutters.
Every day I switched on two sets of limbs,
two sets of eyelids. I summoned double
the will to eat, read the newspaper,
go off to work. The other me kept
wanting to sleep, to curl in the car
of a train going west.
I can't say how this incensed me—
after all I had done for myself—
how, like a child, I needed so much.

II. Songs

Instead of Your Voice

Faced with so much silence from you
I learned to turn everything to sound,
to song, the owls, the church bells,
the gnashing gears of the tractor next door.

Making music from absence of music,
I learned instead the house's breathing,
the muted flap of bat wings outside.
When friends asked my favorite song

I couldn't tell them the one inside me.
I knew what the mind fills in,
what the ear makes from silence—
I kept collecting the vowels of scarcity,
the sounds, the wounds
with the chorus of your silence,
tuning a song I could sing myself in the quiet.

The Song Around Us

Maybe it started in the womb—
the heart's iambic thumps
swish of fluid in the birth sac,
bone pop or hiccup,
the body's syllabics.

Later, as I grew inside her it was
muffled clunk of cowboy boots
jukebox, clip clop of horses,
husk of rabbits scratching straw
snapped bra strap, the cicadas
hysteric acoustics.

Home from Work

Hands glazed with engine oil
or grease from a combine's bearing,
he stood over the sink and scrubbed.
That day was socket wrench and belt tension.
It was turbo-charged and harvest,
shorted out tracer and skid plates.
He'd come home, blood on his flannel,
Coors Light bootlegged in the chain case
of a semi. When his hands were clean
he'd sometimes peel an apple
in one winding ribbon above the sink
while I perched on the countertop watching.
One night in college I crawled into his house
cadaver-white, sick as a dog.
He instructed me to sleep, so I did.
Another night he drove for an hour,
jacking up my car to change a flat.
It was in this way, for years, we kept the myth:
the man could fix anything.

Animal Auctioneer

On the floor, everything was feathers.
Everything was noise and manure tang—
a conveyor belt of boxed animals
moving towards him where
he held court in a wooden booth.
Just below, like a magician,
a lackey yanked out rabbits or
guinea hens and the auctioneer
began the measured beats of his chant
into the half-darkness and as a child
this comforted me. I began to hear it always—
pulse behind chaos. Click of cowboy boots
in two step, rhythmic spit of chew tobacco in a cup.
I would cling to predictability
when all around was hay and mess,
hoof-drag and guttural, birds thrashing
as they were jerked out of boxes.

Adolescence

Deep in the night I would hear it through the wall,
the someone I was becoming.
Until then, a grand pastiche,
I thieved selves from other people—
a look, a demeanor,
lives I thought I wanted.

Of course everything imitates—
the moon siphons light from the sun,
babies make the faces their parents make.
Even Michelangelo practiced forgery:
he aged his Sleeping Cupid in the dirt
like an early grave.

But at night, beyond four walls,
there I almost was—a true thing
I could hear if I listened—
sound instead of echo,
body instead of shadow.

Red Bird

All that's left is Chagall's red bird
suspended over a bouquet,
an embankment, merging with the bodies
of two lovers, blood-colored, levitating over Paris
or, in another scene, riding the bird's back
above Saint-Paul-de-Vence to a table
laden with wine and apples
and the white blade of a knife.
All that's left is to watch its scalloped
feathers become waves, bright nimbus
cradling the lovers. Or the bird hurtling
tail over head, windswept and shedding
its feathers into forest, where they glow,
even dropped from the body they glow,
heralding blessing and doom for the two.
Or the bird perched just beside them,
beating its red wings near the bed
or staring with its one eye,
its beak slightly parted as if to speak.

Country as High Art

Opera is siren and train whistles.
Literature is bar tabs and religious tracks.
Each week, a new installation of white laundry,
perfectly spaced on the line.
Shakespearean tragedy of roadkill,
still life in sidewalk chalk,
patinas of green on copper pipes,
museums of hunting rifles,
and mounted antlers and
fleeting graffiti self-portraits.

How He Survived

That summer, my father dug graves by hand,
twenty-five dollars each. Vietnam
was sending back bodies faster than
they could be buried. He was in college
in a dry town in North Carolina.
Moonshiners sucked white lightning
from mash and heat. Ski slopes
on Sugar Mountain cut like rivers
through the trees. Nixon promised
to bring more boys home, said
I want peace as much as you do,
but they kept coming in boxes,
flag-draped and rolled off planes.
Years later, I watched my father go quiet
when Neil Young climbed the stage
to sing "Ohio" in front of the same flag
and I knew he was back there,
working for hours in the mountain's shadow,
waist-deep in a grave that could have been his.

Midwinter Garden
for Quinn

The garden festooned in light,
my daughter and I wend through hedges.
Luminarias grace the wide lawns,
and every urn and finial stands out in relief
against the gathering dark. It will be weeks
before snow enfolds the landscape—
white layering on the grotto, the knoll,
the tower and carillon.
Still the coming of snow can be felt
as we round the meadow, the wind
bracing, elliptical, sweeping our hair.
A peal of bells hurries us along,
back to the chambered lights
and hidden alcoves. It's late
but we linger on the paths
flanked by cypress and winterberry,
warming our hands by a quiet fire.
Past the arbor, the wind has stilled,
the elm tree is sentinel to the long night,
and we too are witnesses—
shivering, transfixed, set aglow.

III. Thresholds

Yellowstone

What I remember is geyser mist
and bison. That god-awful campsite

they gave us the first night. Stalking
elk behind an outcropping of rock.

Foil potatoes forgotten in the fire. Being
lifted up for a better look.

The unearthly colors of hot springs,
how they sank down into holes

of sinter and blue. Wolves yowling
over the volcanic plain.

The glug and suck of mud pots,
the steam vents flashing water

to vapor. On the lakeshore,
moose tracks hidden in the sand verbena.

Sulfur fog and lodgepole pines
waiting for fire.

Monolith

Along the coast
of central California
the road clung to cliffs
and every twist
wrapped me closer
to earth or closer
to a precipice.
One day I walked
a narrow trail
to the sea
where I fixated
on a monolith
of lonely stone.
A mountain peak
rising from sand,
it cut a shape
on the horizon
I could see
behind my eyelids,
and even now
I see it,
block of lava
rounded by tides,
clung to by limpets
and starfish,
rock that taught me
to be alone.

Seals

In L.A. you said Go, you have a turning lane
and I said No, I don't and you said You do and
you were right about that but I was right
not to trust you. We took a path to the ocean
that was less path than an absence of grass
and we sat above the waves, reading.
Along Route 1 on the beach, fat black seals
looked marooned, though they weren't
and I thought I understood them.
We kept driving and we climbed above Yosemite Falls
where I wanted to lie beside you like seals but you said no.
We raced to the bottom and you buckled into the tent
said you were bone tired even though
you weren't, so I went for a walk. I visited
the bear car—the mangled one put on display
to warn campers that bears
are bears. You spent the night
zipped in that nylon chrysalis,
never emerging, never alighting.
Another day, the gas tank went dry as the climate
and we spun down the hills in neutral, fuming.
In Joshua Tree I spread myself on an outcropping
of white rocks where I thought time wouldn't find me.
Things spoiled—the beer baked
in the backseat and you couldn't love me.
The silence that day still takes up space,
like so much desert humming in the eye.
Back on the coast, I pictured
the gnarled rock faces caving,
whole cliffs careening to the sea,

some glimpsed premonition
of leaving. As our plane lifted,
continent slipped beneath cloud,
and you slept like the cabin
was a great cradle.

The Island

I.

Sliver of skin cut from the mainland,
racked with pallets, crab traps,
and measured in pilings.
You are wing flap, bright stripe
of drawbridge gate,
fat bird I almost smashed
crossing at night,
straight body of egret
flying like an arrow
above the marshes.
Driftwood and slow rust,
tide rise and salty flats.
The church's modest steeple
has eyes in all directions and
mornings the street cleaner sucks and sucks
the curbs until they are burnished
by the tipped and spinning brush.
Trucks roll over the beach,
rods dropped in PVC,
fishermen keeping vigil on the great
spread of the ocean or feeling
the spiked vertebrae of a conch
shell underfoot until a large one
is hoisted up, layers of sand-smooth
strata, its whorled tip like the top
of a minaret.

II.

That morning between storm and blue
below the rusty gutters of the house next door
someone was turning trash—the sharp chemical
reek reminded me some things can never
be burned, they just slip into another form,
metal turning to oxides, plastic turning to
cyanide. Faced with too much fire
we melt into something else.
These flames in my life
lick and lick until I'm burned smooth.
I move through the world
barely parting the air.
I am fire-quick and sand-blasted,
passing like a black cat over the island
slipping under decks and down sidewalks
quiet as a shadow.

III.

White buoys bobbing in the slips beside me
I watched a skiff come in,
twenty gulls diving and lifting above the boat
while the mate dipped a plastic bucket
into the bay and sloshed the deck,
Wire baskets in the truck beds
waiting for the day's catch.

IV.

I walked that morning to Mariner's Point
above the marina, the phragmitis rustled
and sounded like waves,

I watched the crew of Miss Brittany
open the ship, pull out of the harbor
hooks clanking the top of the mast,
the motor thrumming, the men
working efficiently in their plaid shirts,
tiny waves rippling the bay
past the sole fishing shack hoisted on pilings
the weathered wood hanging over the boat's side
its rusted tail following the bow's wake.
Other men checking the traps, skirting the island,
its curves rounding into the bay,
deer tracks in wet sand where a mast
is stuck in the ground like a massive cross.

V.

I was whisked along ocean currents.
I have drifted from home.
I lived through the brine
and wrecks, I watched
other fish flop on the docks
and bloat.
I am sand grain and blood moon—
I am boat lift and oyster bed.
I am flamed memory.

The Cyclist

Cleats bolted to shoes
clipped to pedals,
I go out in early light
spokes spinning,
gears clicking,
wheels shining like metallic suns,
tack across traffic,
grip the drop bar,
listen for the chain to slip,
power into high cadence
anticipate the downward
curves, brake first then
weight the outside pedal,
lean the bike not the body,
bunnyhop over potholes,
handle obstacles,
sewer grates, trolley rails,
car doors, road kill,
slick film of motor oil,
if I hit a bad edge or a glass
sliver it may be a puncture,
a snake bite, a blowout,
a blip in the rim,
and knowing this, believe me,
I look as far down the road
as I can.

The Mind is Like This

A summer creek,
the current wending sideways,
the rocks making slots
the twigs fit through
or don't, debris bottlenecked,
slick leaves pressed together,
gummed up buds of
tulip poplar, muck of
clay, blood-colored,
sucked up by skunk cabbage
and cilia until some threshold
is reached and the gunk
unsticks itself
rushing to rivers,
inlets, estuaries,
just as the mind might
it seems to flow with
the memory of immobility,
quickened by the time it spent
trapped, its paralysis
becoming the ripple
that frees it.

Cabin

At night behind a flimsy plastic window shade
we watched as a stump slathered with bacon grease
lured foxes in. From the truck, we swept fields
with spotlights looking for deer. I learned to see
their green eyes in the false light.
I lived for my father then. I strained all day to spot
the lone elk he so badly wanted to see.
In summer, hummingbirds whirred
at the red feeder the bear pawed down while we
were gone. In the yard, we shot BB guns at cans,
my cousins silent because without practice,
I could hit at every distance and right in the middle.
Our shower was a garden hose rigged to hot
and a watering can that tipped over the back steps
where one night in winter I stood in the steam and heat
and it began to snow. The driving flakes blew past,
sometimes caught in the steam of the shower, and some-
	how
I was not cold, even as the porch steps
were freezing, even in my nakedness.
I saw myself without pretense, the way a fox might see
	itself.
I turned my body toward the white fields
where I followed tracks until they were lost in the creek.
The moon was fixed over the mountain like a great eye.

IV. Visions

Blank Begets Blank

Blank begets blank. Absence begets absence.
　　　　　　—Jasmin Lee Cori

Until it doesn't—each day I undo years of silence with
　　　silence.
I find things like blades, fish bones, red innards
of pomegranate. I hear high heels on laminate,
rush of trucks, squirrel claws, lost sister.

The silence is blank, but not empty— a moment past
nothing a whole world crowds in. Some things I expect:
locked doors and field-stretch. Then the unknown—
helicopter thrashing air over water. Elk lifting its head.

I go into the thing that seems to cripple me. My presence
feels expected. My fears come around like animals
at my feet. My dreams are nothing I recognize.

Ode to Shapeshifters

Slipping between forms

like it's nothing to become

new, as if any one of us

might do the same, you

wake up as one thing and,

as the world clicks

half a degree on its axis,

end up another.

Man-Owl, Deer-Woman,

what magic is it to switch

so quickly to another

existence, survival

the only task

for your days?

What I wouldn't give

to split as you do,

as if from an unseen

chrysalis into a fresh body,

the voice in my head

getting simpler—

I am alive again.

I am alive.

I am.

Girl Become Hawk

My four-year-old daughter is trying on animals for size.
Mantis Shrimp. Buffalo. Honeybee. With each new species
her mind flies to a new reality and suddenly she is stam-
peding across the hardwood or waggling inside a hive of
blankets. Not content to simply bear witness, she becomes,
as Adrienne Rich says, *the thing itself and not the myth.* She
waits for me to catch up—I am not yet one with the crea-
ture. I am lodged in my human existence, unable to slip
from ego and worry. I am eyeing clutter on the coffee table.
I reckon the minutes until lunchtime. Meanwhile, Wobbe-
gong Shark has settled herself into a reef, her fringed skin
blending to seaweed. She sits motionless, except for flicks
of her tail luring in fish and squid. It occurs to me she is
twice hidden: from daughter to shark, from shark to reef,
and all this in the time it takes me to shed the concerns of
selfhood. I learn this from my daughter: how to access an
animal self, an existence not sublimated to so much fuss.
We are about survival: food, defenses, escape. We are blub
and flutter. We are claw and twirl. Now become Hawk,
she catches wind from the ridges. She grinds bones in her
second stomach. She is Mollusk, archaic and plated. She is
Cheetah, her name means spotted one. My identity feels
fixed like hers isn't. Blink and she is another being—mirac-
ulous, inscrutable, bent on staying alive.

On Seeing Pleiades

Somehow the stars are both ice and fire—
seven sisters lodged in the bull's left shoulder.
Parsing this reminds me myths are a bridge we cross over.
The story I told stranded me in a continent of sky. Others
landed some place predictable—a cloud, a moon.

In Australia, the seven stars are ice maidens
who would not warm to mortals.
Even circling a campfire, they barely melted,
their silver hair a carapace of ice on their backs—
a few drops from their cold bodies put out the flames.

And they became stars. The fire they doused
became part of them. Life can be snuffed out
by something that is also life.

Bull of Heaven

Tossing his head over the sky,
he thinks it's his burden
to throw off the dark.
He believes his insistence
brings the sun each morning,
not a brilliant angle that tilts
the world into warmth.
He bucks with his spangled horns
as if, once and for all,
he might gore into brightness,
gouge a hole that will stay
unpatched until light is all there is.
He can't be told this resistance is futile,
for him, it is night or almost night.

The Cowshed

Set off by indigo and right angles
Chagall's cow appears to know
something. He regards me with a
familiarity as he tilts his beveled
head back. There is no moon
at which to bay. He keeps
eyeing me as I peer in the windows
of the shed which could be lined
with jars, mirrors, it's difficult to tell.
Outside, the fields are swept into bands
of cobalt, teal, deep green and he
keeps tipping his chin up,
as if star gazing, his emerald neck
leaner than one might think,
and still he looks at me—he has
to move his pupil back to do it.
Perhaps, I think, he is waiting
for a pause in the talk
in my head, a few beats of silence
so he can say his piece.
I quiet the radio, the fan's static,
my own mind and suddenly,
forever, I know why he stares—
they mean to kill him,
but somehow he goes on living,
sky-drunk, bigger than the house
that's meant to hold him.

Finger Lake

For Isla

The storm gathers behind the red barns—
it sits atop wood piles and hovers above the lake.
Below are trenches dredged by ancient glaciations,
ice slicing shale, ice beveling the ridges where
I stand now in the vineyard, shivering.

It is autumn. The baby is ill, wailing
through the nights. I make my body a stream
she drinks from. Frost settles in the valleys
while the lake's warmth suffuses
the hillsides, sweetening the grapes.

I remember when I was twice-filled with life,
aging my baby nine months like wine.
Our blood pooling in the placental lake,
villi stretching and stretching toward me,
I fed iron and sugar to her nest of veins.

In the morning, the grapes will be cut from the trellises
to be pressed and lose their skins. In time the wine
will taste like honey, apples, wet stones.
For now, we watch the clouds amass—
her pale fingers cluster around mine.

V. Miracles

Settling Down

This house has good bones
despite the rest.

Never mind the mold blooming like a tumor
on the doorframe.

Never mind the way immobility
is so much like a death.

It could be home—
coursed through like blood
in a body cavity—
exploited, returned to.

We could live here,
the walls holding us
like a second skin,
witnesses to the miracles,
the tedium of brushed teeth,
the clock's pulse,
the cicadas intimating
god knows what over and over.

We could turn a corner as slight
as the twist in a double helix,
everything benign and
malignant trapped in one place—
a room,
a home,
this body.

Lumpectomy

The day I blacked out, falling two inches from the sink
into oblivion, the tumor in my right breast scooped out,

the scar like a sad red mouth,
I knew what it was to war with my body.

For months the warm probe orbited my breast
searching for a sick moon caught in the fibrous tissue.

On the ultrasound, the lump was a dark mass
the shape of an artist's palette. Another day

I was awake while the biopsy's hollow needle
pulled out cores the size of rice grains.

Days after surgery, I changed the dressing
and braced myself for a bloody ordeal.

But the gauze was clean and at the site
of the exhumed tumor were

tape strips spaced in white lines,
like war paint, along my ribs.

Ode to Liminality

Ode to shadows

ode to almost

ode to not yet

ode to unknown.

Ode to both

ode to thresholds

ode to windows

ode to outposts

ode to roads.

Ode to fault lines

ode to hallways

ode to margins

ode to coasts

ode to limbo

ode to alleys

ode to ghosts.

Class Reunion

I wasn't there. I heard you met
at the Goodwill Fire Station
and across the alley in the parking lot,
as if ten years had not passed,
kegs were strapped on the truck beds
and Clayton Smith's tires were slashed.
Trouble is, nothing ever happened in this town
except what we made happen. Most of us
left. We all had to drive past that godforsaken
metals factory on the way to our futures. The flat
sweep of fields, the horizon's limitlessness
was not promising. I remember
on drunk driving day the fire company
snuck a smashed car onto the grass
at the high school. As we filed into the parking lot
someone screamed, recognizing a face.
On the lawn, three of our classmates sprawled
death-white and bloodied, thrown from the car
that was lit on fire. Girls wept while the hoses
doused the scene, their friends still not moving,
while the boys said *It's a trick* which of course
it was. Like I said, nothing ever happened.
The stadium had no memory of us.
The hallways didn't echo our voices back.
So it makes sense that tires were slit,
in a town like this where the most you can do
is keep someone else from leaving.

County Fair

I.

Every summer it rose up like Atlantis
out of an ocean of corn fields,
blinking its round bulbs into the night.
Noosed with glow necklaces
we plunk goldfish with ping pong balls,
flush them into plastic bags.
When the heavy music of the carousel
stops, we crowd the silence with voices
until the thick brass and percussion thumps
the air again and the horses spin. Nearby
a clown is strangling balloons into animals.

II.

What we see first is Madison Murray,
with her midriff out in front of God
and everybody. For some,
this is as good as it gets.
Inside the Gravitron
pressed and levitating
around spinning walls,
somehow we don't collide,
each of us held by the same force
in different places.
Back outside, the lights echo
in faces, the carousel's Wurlitzer
womps and womps in our chests.
We know there is nothing

in this town for us. We disappear
in the woods awhile, but can't escape it—
everything, the blurred horses,
the bodies sinking back
to earth, everything says
we are still here.

III.

When the booths go dark on the last night
we stay to watch them tear it down—
the tents collapsing, the Octopus retracting
 its metal limbs. We watch as the cars
of the Ferris Wheel are stacked like cups,
its rim unhinged, its broken curves folding.
The carousel's horses are herded into
trailers, its gilded panels stacked
like playing cards and carried off.
They dismantle our lost city,
the rides are worlds closed in
on themselves and racked on trucks.
And what can we do but watch,
struck as we are by this one fact—
how quickly and without ceremony
it is all undone.

Dear Calendula

Calendula is derived from the Latin kalends, *which means the first day of the month*

Dear little clock, dear calendar,
I might have known things wouldn't last.
To believe the myths, in your face
I might divine the weather,
a true match, the holy light
encircling Mary.
Dear dark heart, dear sticky nimbus,
he was cruel, but he was alive.
He had not yet stepped from the river's
current. He had not yet turned the knife
on himself.
Dear honey-colored, dear tincture,
I knew so little in that season—
Dear prophet-blossom, dear fallen sun,
he always smelled like you.

Skunk Hollow

After we were broken irreparably,
I went to the creek. I was always going
To creeks in the face of loss as if things
Might be mended there by geology.

Except I had no sense of place. I might
Have started with the remains of a mill
Nearby, three hundred years old and still.
No water bringing the wheel to life,

No wheat abraded by the pair of stones—
They lay in the sun turned upward like eyes.
The mill stood indifferent to time while
I tried to make sense of being alone.

I was trying to parse how we split
Like two limbs of a tree. I got nowhere.
Like sound, the blame ricocheted here, there—
Yes, we were hollow. Yes, we were careless.

It took time for me to get my bearings,
But I kept coming back to this—the mill,
The creek, the stones kept apart by skill
Or luck, the wheel causing water to sing.

In theory, we could still go back and revise
the story: I gave you what I was able.
What you took from me was a miller's toll—
the portion of bread that kept you alive.

The Light Inside

The light inside is broken but I still work.
I carry my dark down halls, fields,
it is shut up in my bones' cold locker.
Somehow the days pass. I stand in a room
with my broken light, among all these others
carrying their dark, and yet I persist.
My blood thrusts as it should down the corridors of veins.
Even without brightness the body asserts itself,
sopping up oxygen, flinging platelets,
the heart's metered spasms keeping rhythm
in the shadow of the ribcage.
Even after great loss, brain tissue lifted out
or uterus removed, there are the stunning
resiliencies of flesh. Even after death,
filaments stiffening into rigor, in a few days
cell walls give way and enzymes slip like moons
into cytoplasm, freeing the ligaments.
It took many years to realize
I could learn to see this as miracle—
how the body sometimes goes on
despite everything.

Map Song

Australia's indigenous peoples use songlines, which are
song cycles passed down from the Spirit Beings, to navi-
gate vast terrain and identify sacred landmarks.

I.

First you should know
you can sing your way back.

Say you've rounded a bend
you don't recognize—

Say the thread of trail you're on
disappears.

Terrain wells up around you
becoming a trap
or a puzzle.

Mountains blur and collapse,
losing their names.

The twist of the river
suggests nothing;

there is no pattern
in the trees.

II.

I know a people
who embed their maps in song.

They sing their way back,
as the landscape balks—
as it veils itself in shadow and light.

The song is a relic,
it leads to the ridgeline—
it rises up and knows where it's going.

III.

Ahead, there are signs we can't distinguish,
the earth waits to be known.
We keep singing.

www.ingramcontent.com/pod-product-compliance
Lightning Source LLC
Chambersburg PA
CBHW030856090426
42737CB00009B/1245